Time and Tide

Shed Poets

Boland Press

Boland Press
Grove Mill
Hollyfort
Co. Wexford
http://bolandpress.blogspot.com

A CIP catalogue record for this book
is available from the British Library

ISBN: 978-1-907855-12-2

The Shed Poets gratefully acknowledge
financial assistance from
Dun Laoghaire-Rathdown County Council

Cover mosaic reproduced by kind permission of the
children of Ballymoney with Karin Dubsky
and Blinda Moller

Cover design by Boland Press

Printed in Ireland by
SPRINT-Print

The Shed Poets Society
meets each week in a
terraced garden that
overlooks Killiney Bay.
Time and Tide is the
group's fifth collection
of poetry.

Acknowledgement is given to the following publication where some of these poems, or versions of them, have appeared:

Music in Stone by Maureen Perkins
(Boland Press)

Foreword

In the property world 'Location' we are told is the magic word. In the realm of poetry it could be just as important. Once I visited the Poets' Shed perched as it is on a clifftop ledge overlooking Killiney Bay. Here in this idyllic location the poets meet every week to write and read their poetry, to polish and perfect it.

This collection is reflective, as befits the writings of a group of women with such a wide, varied and rich life experience spanning as it does most of the last century. They have known love and loss, have endured tragedy and frugal times and yet have retained their good humour and capacity to enjoy life.

Bernie Kenny finds joy in an 'ordinary and amazing day' is positive about 'things not to do before I die'. Says a 'thankful prayer for a long life/ so many friends, so much love' and she can even look forward in 'Going Green' to an eco-friendly funeral 'in a wicker coffin or a shroud' and lie in 'my graveyard, a wild flower/ meadow in Wexford County'.

Maureen Perkins has a very seeing eye. On a London bus journey she chronicles the landmarks as she passes, notes the National Gallery and the 'wing paying tribute to Da Vinci' whom she describes as 'a bit of a dandy' whose 'elusive genius penetrates with a quill'

> 'a foetus in the womb, a revelation,
> the story of betrayal at the Last Supper
> told by gestures. The wing of a bird
> his dream of flight.'

Maureen even mines a Garda barracks for poetic content, the young recruit 'missing the shelter of drumlin country *and the hiss of the tilley'* and *'obeys new masters who/ break their own rules'*.

We are brought back to childhood with **Marguerite Colgan's** poem 'Samhain', *'apples bob on water . . . the splashing, the cheering . . . our mam joining in the fun'* and then a change of mood

> *'Next evening we do the rounds in the Church*
> *whispers of earnest prayers inside, the shuffle*
> *out into the mist, back again, shoals of us*
> *in and out praying for our dead.'*

In 'A Curious Walk', among other perils, Marguerite encounters a black dog *'I talk, talk to him,/ talk him down,/ pass,/ leave him behind his garden wall,/ raging barks fainting in the bright sunlight'*.

It only takes eight short verses for **Judy Russell** to give us a word picture of her life. 'Consequences' tells us the story of a war baby who in adult life *'always lived in places with potential'*. Now she says

> *'Not again. I've grown roots. Planting food*
> *settles me, hawthorn and crab-apple*
> *grow wild around my home.'*

There are glimpses of Spartan living, the generosity of country folk. Judy's lyrical voice breaks out in 'Dawn Song', she writes *'the thornbush pierced with rags'* and

> *'shoals of tumbling crows*
> *clutter the strident morn*
> *while a cloud like the smile on a dolphin's face*
> *licks across the dawn.'*

Rosy Wilson is a philosophical about ageing *'beliefs I've held so firmly dissipate'* and *'Maybe I listen more . . . hug tree trunks wider than my arms embrace'*. She quotes a Zen monk who values Understanding over Knowledge because it *'is a river, always finds a way/ flows over stones/ meanders around boulders.'*

Rosy shares with Judy a liking for water themes, in 'Unchartered Waters' Judy writes, 'small boats nudge/ against the stone pier' and in 'Atonement'

> *'. . . she opens a door*
> *in the sea, and slides between*
> *the silky billows, smiling.'*

Many of Rosy's poems have this same connection with water

> *'he tells her not to swim against the current*
> *she insists she will float with the tide'.*

'April Sequence' opens with *'waves at Clahane had never been so blue'* and in a later verse *'my toes are pellucid as I tread water'*. Another of her poems is titled 'In darkness and water we arrive', and 'Befogged on a Beach' includes the verse

> *'in up to his waist*
> *kick-splash, stone-throws*
> *early miracle merging*
> *of air with ocean'.*

Carol Boland has a subtle style. We wonder what is the story behind 'Pulling her Strings' and 'Faces'. We can picture the pair in 'Coupling' so young sounding, so sassy and then we feel the chill of 'So this is what death looks like'

      'a slow regression into nothingness'.

Still we find solace in the tenacity of 'The Willow Tree' even though it had been felled three times by storms and though

> *'It would be simpler to put*
> *the half-life out of its misery*
> *had not the buds persisted'*

and eventually

> *'a site sheltered from the north wind*
> *opens up possibilities*
> *and freshly dug earth accepts*
> *stake and stem*
> *supporting each other*
> *in a fresh bed'*

which brings us neatly back to 'Location'.

This is a lovely collection of poems. I have enjoyed reading every one of them and heartily recommend them to the readers.

Mamo McDonald
November 2015

Tell me, what is it you plan to do
with your one wild and precious life?
— Mary Oliver

CONTENTS

Bernie Kenny

Carol Boland

Marguerite Colgan

Maureen Perkins

Rosy Wilson

Judy Russell

Time and Tide

Bernie Kenny holds an MA in
Creative Writing. Her published
books include *A Walk in Dalkey,
Always Dalkey Always the Sea*
and *These are my Days*

After the Deluge

All yesterday and through fractured night
the storm boomed, a monster ruled our world,
shattered branches, scattered limbs of trees,
thundered a deafening drumbeat in the air.
Rain crashed down in torrents, sent man
and beast shuddering for shelter, burst
river banks, made lakes of meadows,
seeped under doors and flooded streets.

Dawn pierces cloudy darkness, colours return
changing with the light. Trees drip a sibilant
percussion and mushrooms, pink, brown,
lethal white break through the forest floor.
By mid-morning as the sun climbs high
our earth rejoices.

Bernie Kenny

Dawn Walk

This May morning calls me
to take a pebbled path
to Annaghmakerrig lake.

Lonely and level as glass
still water reflects tall pines,
mirrors a steel-grey sky.

Silence is barely broken
by my crunching feet
and the first voice of a nameless bird.

Above, below, all around,
nothing but miracles:
daisies open sleep-drowned eyes;

bluebells shimmer in dewy clumps;
white butterflies flit
from bell to nectar'd bell

living a short life to the full;
shy primroses reveal pale yellow,
lovelier than shining buttercups.

Tiny blooms, speedwell, vetch, wild
strawberry say, look at me,
I look, breathe freshness, largesse

happy to be here, at one
with our dazzling transient world
on this ordinary amazing day.

Longevity

In colourful profusion, hyacinths, narcissi,
yellow tulips, a flowering cactus
fill all my vases. The mirrored
sideboard doubles as an altar
and, like incense, floral perfume
a thankyou prayer for long life,
so many friends, so much love.

We sit at a round table
a centrepiece of white roses,
cutlery, folded napkins, clink of glasses,
spangles of laughter and smiling
faces meeting, greeting, how have you
been – did you hear – you don't look
a day older – and for me
congratulations
as if I had reached my ninetieth
year on merit rather than
a gift of days to live, to love,
be grateful, be delighted.

John
For Mary Ann

I sing a hymn of praise and thanks
for our beloved John, a truly good man,
one of the best, greatly missed.

He lived only for Mary Ann,
his treasured wife, for Owen and Gareth,
their more than precious boys.

John left a legacy of love,
abundant love. And you may ask
where does all that love go.

It doesn't go. We pray that, in time,
grief and pain of loss grow less
while love remains, lives on, will never die.

Bernie Kenny

Od age

has suddenly caught up with me.
At ninety, I'm not half the woman
I was at eighty-nine, when to walk

to stride three miles or more
on Dalkey's gentle hills
was a pleasure.

Now instead what I love best
on chair or couch or bed
is rest, blissful, easeful rest.

As my tireless pen spells words
on the blank page I ask
is this a poem, will there be more.

While I breathe, love, am loved
am at peace and blessed
my ordinary life becomes a poem.

Bernie Kenny

Going Green

Although I do not own a field
nor patch of grass, in my paved
terraced garden I'll keep bees,
my pot-planted flowers will bloom,
organic raspberries crop profusely
and there will be honey, jars and jars.

To save electricity I will use
a slow-cooker, tasty casseroles
will greet me at evening
as I come weary in the door
or for a super-fast repast I'll find
my long-discarded pressure-cooker.

I will recycle diligently,
unplug electrical devices at night,
install a solar panel, sell my car,
walk, take public transport,
go vegetarian once a week or more,
knit, sew, mend and darn

and at the end,
in a wicker coffin or a shroud
I'll have an eco-friendly funeral
at our new green burial ground,
my graveyard a wild flower
meadow in Wexford County.

Things Not To Do Before I Die

I will not
read Ulysses
nor the Complete Works

queue to view the Mona Lisa
when I could sit by the Seine

learn to bake a meringue roulade
you would love my Eton mess

abseil, bungee jump, scuba-dive
risk kicking the bucket list

and be no longer able
to cherish family and friends

always grateful
for love, long life, lazy days.

Carol Boland is a performance
poet and Poetry Therapy
Practitioner. Her books include
The Overture and *Hostage*

The Coupling

She carries him
     in the folds of her dress
     crease of her elbow
     smile of her hips
or knotted fast in the roots
of her jet hair
like a child's comb.

He carries her
     in the blue of his jeans
     the furrow of his brow
     pride of his shoulders
or bedded in his lyrics
on white sheets
strewn across the day.

The Willow Tree

Three times the willow tree
stood against the storm
and three times
the wind felled it
ripping fibrous roots
from the Wexford soil,
its canopy of twigs
flying above slated ground
crashing down like
an upturned umbrella.

It would be simpler to put
the half-life out of its misery
had not the buds persisted.

As the wind drops
a site sheltered from the north wind
opens up possibilities
and freshly dug earth accepts
stake and stem
supporting each other
in a fresh bed.

Pulling Her Strings

She was a marionette
a teller of stories
by attachment
controlled
by a disembodied voice
pressing buttons
from behind
a velvet curtain

      until she found
a pair of scissors
and once again
the stage was hers.

So this is what death looks like

a slow regression
into nothingness
like her wedding ring
slipping off her bony finger
her refusal of a poached egg
a sip of tea.

Hope crumbles bread
left on a hospital tray
wheeled across
a bed of crowded memories
that spring to life
in bursts of laughter
thrown to visitors
perched like swallows
with a promise to return.

Carol Boland

Moving the dream on

It took me twenty years
to climb the attic stairs
twenty years of
poetry, spells
and sound cures
to ease a wheezing chest.

It was waiting for me
by the water tank
a turquoise shell
silver locked with
a handle stout enough
to hold a young girl's dream.

A traveller, I carried this case
from Dublin to London
rented flats to owner-occupieds
Tunbridge Wells to Wexford
packed each attic with strings of time
watching it, watching me
dance around its hinges.

Today I wipe the skin of dust
from my over-weight luggage
heave it down the stairs
unpack your love-blue letters
and carefully unfold them,
read and shred.

What is it that makes us

lead
while being wounded
makes heel
go down
before the ball
one twisted ankle
at a time.

And what is it that makes us
invite flies to settle
in our sores
offer them a home
in which to multiply.

In the balance of this life
the wounded and healed
share a meal
hold hands beneath
the table.

Faces

long   cold
vacant
washed out
from the outpouring
thin
young men
shadows of yesterday

jaws   shoulders
straining
from the weight
of his coffin
empty of what made him
outstanding

his heart, eyes, lungs
now filling
hopes of others

leaving
the mourners
memories
of his easy smile.

Marguerite Colgan is a member of Bealtaine Writers. Her first collection of poetry will be published in 2016.

Achill's Watercolour

Heatherpurple ices grassgreen
holds ceannabhán lights
on bog, soft as chocolate fudgecake,
sliced, laid out to dry turfbrown,

a tent of blue above sings larksong
dyes the ocean seagreen, seablue
races tumbling over the sand,

Sliabhmore, stonewashed denim
with boulder knots and speckled
sheepwhite, sheepblack,

lowering clouds smoulder grey
rainbow rises from the wave, arcs
red orange yellow green blue indigo violet
echoes a return
violet indigo blue green yellow orange red.

Samhain

Out of school in October, my brother Ed
and I journey with our mam,
no memory of hackney, train or bus
over the Sound to our grandparents
in Achill.

Turf blazes on a low hearth in the dark kitchen
crowded with cousins, talk is peppered with
Irish words, maistín, geidhimín.
Uneasy I'm all ears, all eyes.

That night and a tin bath is carried in after tea,
apples bob on water, ruffle the sparkle of lamplight,
the splashing, the cheering, cries of foul,
Ed trying and vying with the others,
our mam joining in the fun.

Next evening we do the rounds in the Church
whispers of earnest prayers inside, the shuffle
out into the mist, back again, shoals of us
in and out praying for our dead.

We visit our kith and kin in daylight mist,
tea, currant cake, sometimes a thruppence,
everyone knows Maggie Ned,
our mam is Peggy to our dad.

Marguerite Colgan

Transfers in the Dark

The wet night plays watercolours
on wet roads, footpaths, headlights
search ahead with monster eyes,

high orange lights show strings
of rainbeads, slanting falling,
uncounted, uncountable,

umbrellas sway rainbows under
a loaded sky, she's forgotten hers.
Rain silvers down her coat,

spangles her red hat, yellow scarf,
as she dances along the pavement,
boots click, splashing, cracking

glass puddles to smithereens.
She turns the key, steps inside,
closes the door on the raindrops,

hangs her hat, her scarf, slips off
the boots, they turn again to clothes

against the cold wet night.

Travelling On

1

Under a blanket of morning blush
a sash of yellow ochre binds sky and land.
Across the wide arc two jet streams
on a journey as a new day unrolls.

2

A rush of cars choke
the roundabout,
night fog hangs
drying out in the sun

3

Pupils spill from buses, plaid skirts, back packs,
coloured folders close to their chests,
they glide in pairs, whispers spelling the anticipation.

4

One man walked for months, for hours,
last shilling in his pocket
to start his new life, reek of fish on the crowded deck
each wave rolling them nearer the goal,
they see a large vessel, a saviour,
rush of excitement tilts the old wooden boat and
hundreds drown. Did he see the bright light,
did he walk that tunnel to another life.

5

It's April and the swallows have returned.

6

I held my baby, told her to look
to remember that morning,
there was a man walking on the moon
and we were watching.

7

Cows stir and lift from steaming night-shapes
stream up Cnocnashee, a steady plod
on the well-trodden path, one pauses
to grasp a fresh tuft, falls in again,
they scatter on the summit.

8

I'm visiting my sister today, seated among strangers,
now a stranger to herself,
flashes of the girl she was light and fade.
She has forgotten the days, the years
that brought her to here.

A Curious Walk

I turn left, stride
up the long grey ribbon
edged with sungreen
all eyes on me at the gate,
a herd of Charlois bullocks edge closer,
the forwards
and the eyes over the shoulder,
fifteen pairs.
I move,
they turn an arc,
regroup the ruck,
stare silently.

Left again at the drumlin top,
the church ahead,
to get there I must pass
the black dog,
growling, snarling,
coming for me.
I will not let him touch me,
take me over.
I talk, talk to him,
talk him down,
pass,
leave him behind his garden wall,
raging barks fainting in the bright sunlight.

Water playing music to itself

The pipe sings the drumlin tune
notes falling from its mouth
plink-plink plink plonk
into the bed of settled drops.

The chamber, an old cistern
cement of lime and gravel moulded
to a cist holding precious water,
half buried behind the big house

rain water, spring water
playing music to itself
a tumble tune giggles, gurgles
all through the day, all night

two small windows, latticed
with rusting iron, light this cavern
I peer inside sing my wonder
and echo calls it back.

Marguerite Colgan

The Wonder

hair grows and bones, nails
inside organs work without my timetable
I fuss to dress the outside

I can colour me
beautiful carmine lips, fake tan
feel the heat, the cold

wet to the skin
wool fleece, blue silk, cotton thread soaked
no raindrop seeps inside

I cannot see in
but there's a mood, a hunger, rage,
memories, a plan.

Maureen Perkins is a
founder member of Bealtaine
Writers and has an M.A. in
Creative Writing from Queens
University. Her book, *Music in
Stone* was published in 2013.

Columbine

Down the dripping lane to the hazel wood
I stop, startled as two pigeons burst
from a tree exploding skywards –
my eye follows their smack and flap.

They plunge onto a green-grass clearing,
step ungainly in a fantail flare,
side-step, waddle a dance apart,
come close to coo and nibble.

On white-wing flash they fly to roost
in a shower-drenched cypress tree.
Puffball breasts thrust out, they
nod and natter, peck and patter.

Down the dripping lanes today
blood marks a breast, a black eye stares.

Da Vinci

Because of Leonardo and an oyster card
I'm on a bus from Pimlico through Westminster.
Here on such a balmy night Mrs Dalloway dined.
Cabs stream in the blue light
couples dally, drink at street tables,
Nelson soars in Trafalgar Square.

The National Gallery stone white
like a lighthouse, a wing paying
tribute to Da Vinci – the court painter
to the Duke of Milan, a bit of a dandy.
In his garden-vineyard he sees into
the heart of his vines.

These drawings are his memoir,
bursts of activity, arms folded,
Leonardo's elusive genius penetrates
with a quill, see it do it
a foetus in the womb, a revelation,
the story of betrayal at the Last Supper
told by gestures. The wing of a bird
his dream of flight.

Leaving Brighton
After John Constable

Blackbat sky over Brighton beach
time for him to dodge its shallow
fashion, return to wallow in Suffolk
clouds, fleecy as its sheep,

time to see his russet mill house
burnish the tow path to the lock,
froth skimming water, its brim
a sluice gate ready to spill,

time to savour the lighterman
hoist an anchor by the River Stour,
to pencil sketch The White Horse
in the bow-well of his barge.

Barrack Orderly
In memory of John McGahern

They hand out the dull grey rug
initialled with g and a date
its hair chaffs a raw recruit
on duty at night in
the sob of the lamplight
missing the shelter of drumlin
country and the hiss of the tilly.

A blue-serge man silver-buttoned
obeys new masters who
break their own rules.

Polly Perkins
For my daughter Joanne

Icicles hang on the window pane
and Polly in jodhpurs
fills some oats in a pail
stretches to unlock the tack-room door.

Yellow sun glows on the cutstone gable
Lugnaquilla glimmers in its snowy thatch.
In high riding boots she runs to the stable,
cold hands grip the frosted latch.

A handful of oats for her Adonis
sunlight slants in a ray of gold
gripping his forelock, she his Venus,
jumps on his back and away they go.

I stand entranced under the stable awning
hear them gallop into the winter morning.

Maureen Perkins

End of September

From the four corners of the wind,
Achill and Aran, Nephin and Muckish,
they travel in clusters, swapping symptoms,
boosting each other on their hesitant road
to the leafy suburb, where friends
of St. Luke's offer hope,
dry leaves and chestnuts crush under their feet.

Atlantic waves splash in the welcoming voice
of a white-coated nurse from the west.
She shows them their rooms where they rest
till the treatment begins in the clinic nearby.
Fears now diminished
they slope through the path,
dry leaves and chestnuts crush under their feet.

John King from Killalla,
his hair bleached by spray.
The life of the party waits in Wing A,
tattoos on his loins he lies on a table
longs for his fishing boat tied in the bay,
eddies of water lap under his feet.

Jack White comes from under Ben Bulben,
a whale of a man, he walks tall like a cowboy
in brown leather boots, his eyes smiling blue
and his beard like silk. Now bound by ice sheets
unable to sleep, he's back on his farm
loping its hills, a shepherd to his sheep,
gorse and heather crush under his feet.

Boyne Bridge

Like swan wings stretched,
the new bridge rises, sheet white
looking east to the sea,
sky and river horizon hinged.

Standing above the reed beds
and the flora of Yellow Island,
it bends into the sprawling valley,
once the battleground of kings.

Under floodlight at night,
the ghosts of Newgrange ponder
this wonder, a beacon for travellers:
swanknight of the Boyne.

Rosy Wilson is a published
poet and active member of
poetry groups in Dublin and
London. She has published
five collections of poetry.

Yew Tree Walk

We lean on the two thousand year old tree
fit foreheads, breasts, tired thighs on rough bark,
in crevices of its enormous trunk that hold
our cracking bones, our ageing limbs

breathe in scent of resin, feel soft mulch
of leaves strewn underfoot, partake
in their longevity and strength, these
ancient branches sheltering us today

then move slowly under Gothic arches
a pathway planted in the Middle Ages
foliage converges overhead, sun-rays shimmer
the way light permeates old stained glass windows.

April Sequence

1
sunshine paints wide skies
waves at Clahane have never
been so blue

2
a hare lopes across fields
leaps ditches, the heron
lands, hunches shoulders, I lean
on my cane on the bridge
over River Deelagh –
these are my prayers

3
he says 'don't jump in'
she says 'I will swim'

4
the story is . . .

5
only seventeen when Euri joined the partisans
fighting with Tito in the mountains for la Resistenza
contra Mussolini's fascists

6
on the old Yugoslavia coast
my toes are pellucid as
I tread water

7

11th April might have been
our 49th wedding anniversary
I carry flowering currant, rosemary

8

he tells her not to swim against the current
she insists she will float with the tide

9

all the walls of EuriAlda's apartment
are covered with his paintings
her face, her pointed breasts
are his images, vibrant colours
shout her praises

10

in Kilmacreahy cemetery
I place a vase of daffodils on
my husband's Atlantic grave

11

a sheepdog follows
a string of Frisian cows
along the lanes

12

will you come
when the day
is ended.

Perception

Growing older I know less, remember less,
lose my glasses, gloves, the mobile phone,
forget books I'm reading, people's names,
lines of poems, Yeats', Mimi's, my own,

beliefs I've held so firmly dissipate,
the history of my land becomes uncertain,
views I used to promulgate are clouded now
grown fuzzy round the edges.

Maybe I listen more, see daffodils
in hedgerows, a goldfinch in the evening,
hug tree trunks wider than my arms' embrace
or slender stems, turn over autumn leaves.

A Zen monk writes how knowledge resembles
blocks of ice which stop water flowing, while
understanding is a river, always finds a way,
flows over stones, meanders around boulders.

Lunacy

A full moon shines on Annaghmakerrig Lake
claire de la lune, an gealach, la luna chiara,

we listen, water - acqua, uisce, l'eau - splashes
gravel, lake-weed, plucking strings of foam,

plays music on the shoreline we step over
garlanded, bewitched by moonlit water.

A second moon is settled in the depths
diving in we catch a dozen circles tumbling

like golden sovereigns from a slot machine,
sparks like fireflies scoot across the surface,

engulfed in chiaroscuro we emerge
wearing moon-necklaces like strings of pearls.

Rosy Wilson

In darkness and water we arrive

We all start there
darkness
of mother's womb
amniotic sea
breaking waters
flushing
pushing
forcing
birth

emigrants
returning on
the night mailboat
down below
pints of Guinness
rebel songs
cattle rustle
in the hold
up on deck
we watch lights
as we sail
on dark water

Rosy Wilson

Ireland's Eye
Howth
Ringsend
Dun Laoghaire piers
open arms
docking

clanging gangways
waves of welcome
nearly home
though never
the same again.

Rosy Wilson

Befogged on a Beach
weather abroad or weather
in the heart alike come on.
From *Storm Warnings* by Adrienne Rich

We drive from green hills where
sun lights on wild flowers
impatient to throw ourselves
under bright turquoise water

on the brow of Bray Head
our outlook is shrouded
with red mist obscuring
landscape and sky

but strong sun wins through
shines on blue-again sea
we dive in head-first
clean bracing waves

    our toddler returns
    again and again
    holding our hands
    bringing us with him

    in up to his waist
    kick-splash, stone-throws
    early miracle merging
    of air with ocean

Rosy Wilson

we dress on the beach
consider our plans for
life-changes, coffee –
a white mist rolls in

this evening the whole coast
and mountains are coated
dripping-grey fog – young people
reported, lost on the strand.

Rosy Wilson

In the Mendip Hills

following cracks and folds
of an old map, we search for
Stanton Drew, Neolithic site
near a lake in the Chu Valley,

walk through a kissing gate
onto a wide plain, poplars all around,
where the Great Circle is laid:
limestone columns alternate
with pavements holding
pools of water,

a sacred place where Druids perform
ceremonies, Celts come to pray.
The sun is setting, red light
streaks the sky, grandchildren
play hide-and-seek, dodging
from pillar to post.

I stand a little apart
leaning on my cane, enthralled
by mysteries of this ancient scene
pray to spirits of the Valley, settle
within the Circle's symmetry.

Judy Russell is a poet and
playwright. She has published
two collections of poetry,
Wind Horses and *Glencree
Riverain* (Lapwing).

On a summer morning

when they first found you
in the Phoenix Park under a rusty bush
head bedded down on a green fleece

they could not find your name nor purse,
didn't know you were a mother
dreaming a future for your children

books, education, all those possibilities
to send back home to Timisoara.

Judy Russell

Nancy Maude Campbell 1887 - ?

There was a time when hooves of cows and calves
and sturdy pony trampled the emerging ferns.

You met him in London, married the rebel poet
who fed your notions of freedom, brought you here
to the wildness of the Wicklow mountains, a man
who dreamed beauty out of the land. Yourself a poet
you backed the Irish Volunteers, saw Joseph arrested,
imprisoned for seventeen months, leaving you
with your republican ideals, the farm to work, children
your labour and comfort, the hired hand
the undoing of a troubled marriage.

The blackthorn leaves in the haggard
are not open yet, but a blaze of white star petals
shoot from the branches, hiding needle thorns.

Atonement

A woman called Memory
digs a hole under a rose tree
puts in a sack of jaded hopes

out-dated keepsakes
a bunch of sour grapes,
her darkest night

fills in the pit with dusters,
burnt sponge cakes, cracked
fingers. Brushing crumbs

from her knees she opens a door
in the sea, and slides between
the silky billows, smiling.

Judy Russell

On half an acre

The cottage lay derelict, empty
except for the raddled ram
cudding in the hearth

since the family packed up,
moved to a new council house
two mountains away

leaving the timber chimneypiece,
tarred crane, curled pothooks
still fit for purpose.

Strangers came, made welcome
by neighbours glad to see smoke
tilting from the chimney

gifting eggs wrapped singly
in newspaper, a bag of turf,
fresh milk in a soda bottle.

A few years on, struggling
to make a living, and they're gone,
leaving marigolds seeding
in a kettle at the door.

Uncharted waters

Crystal clear water
green to the sandy floor
shifts seaweed among
lichen-gold rocks
crusted with mussels.

Small boats nudge
against the stone pier,
empty moorings bob
where once the *Lazy Daisy*
turned with the tide

and keeping faith
I rowed out to sea,
baby stowed at my feet,
three boys trailing fingers
in curling waves.

Judy Russell

Consequences

1

There's such relief
dancing in the streets
a conga snaking through Piccadilly.

2

Ruin and rubble all over Europe
and the dead are so many.
In Berlin women pick up shovels,
use bare hands, begin.

3

Early fog swallows landing strips
laid along a field where Grandpa and me,
heads down, pick pearly mushrooms.

4

As the labour of peace begins
in Europe another race suffer reprisals,
victims become persecutors.

5

We move house, the war baby
and parents camp inside potential,
fixing it up. Siblings return, four years
fostered in New Jersey, a long time
away for ones so young.

6

At nineteen my brother emigrates
to America, my sister travels the world.

7

In adult life I've always lived in places
with potential. After a few years
of fixing up, we'd move.

8

Not again. I've grown roots. Planting food
settles me, hawthorn and crab-apple
grow wild around my home.

Dawn song

Scud like a black swan's outstretched wing
unfurls above the crags
and the sky is blue and the sky is pitch
the thornbush pierced with rags

shoals of tumbling crows
clutter the strident morn
while a cloud like the smile on a dolphin's face
licks across the dawn.